Disparate Kind

Neurodivergent Poets Chapbook No. 1

Published in collaboration with The Neurodivergent Student Project
University of California Santa Barbara
Copyright © Snowy Plover Press 2026

ISBN # (print) 978-0-9669232-1-6
ISBN # (ebook) 978-0-9669232-2-3

Editor
Yvette Doss

Associate Editors
Shanna Killeen
Zoe Sage
Luu Pham

Cover art: Aerialist with balloon (c. 1850) by Unknown.

Disparate Kind (ISBN) is published by Snowy Plover Press in collaboration with the Neurodivergent Student Project at University of California Santa Barbara. Please address all correspondence to: editor@snowyploverpress.com. All poems are works of the imagination. Disparate Kind features poetry by poets who identify as neuro-divergent. Submissions accepted via email only at this time. Disparate Kind accepts simultaneous submissions, however all work must be original and unpublished in print or online. Please withdraw work that has been accepted for publication elsewhere. For more information, contact the editor via editor@snowyploverpress.com

Contents

POEMS

Contents

SUBMIT

TO DISPARATE KIND:
NEURODIVERGENT POETS
CHAPBOOK NO 2

*EMAIL UP TO 5 POEMS TO
EDITOR@SNOWYPLOVERPRESS.COM
SEE FULL SUBMISSION DETAILS AT
SNOWYPLOVERPRESS.COM

Editor's Note

Welcome to the first issue of Disparate Kind: Neurodivergent Poets Chapbook. The idea began with a simple goal, to gather neurodivergent poets in one place. As I spent time with every submission, immersing myself in each poem's world, I saw this publication take shape into what I hoped it would be, a place where neurodivergent poets could recognize themselves in the company of others.

The name Disparate Kind grew out of that intention. "Kind" refers to kinship, to writers who understand what it feels like to think a little differently, notice a little differently, and write from that place. What connects the work in this issue is a sense of belonging among writers who rarely appear together in the same publication.

When the call when out, I did not know who would answer. What arrived were strong submissions from across the United States, Canada, and Latin America, from poets of all ages and backgrounds.

What they share is an impulse toward honesty. They write clearly, directly, powerfully. Reading them felt like finding people who speak in neighboring dialects of the same interior language.

Several poets wrote with attention to sensory detail and precision that honors our divergent ways of processing. Others traced memory, joy, or self-understanding. A few surprised me with their humor; others with the quiet steadiness of their voice. Across the issue, the poems approach their subjects with unmistakable directness and power.

This first issue brings these voices together so that they can stand alongside one another and build kinship through the simple fact of being here, of belonging here. I am grateful to the poets who trusted us with their work and grateful to you for opening these pages.

Warmly,
Yvette Doss
Editor
editor@snowyploverpress.com

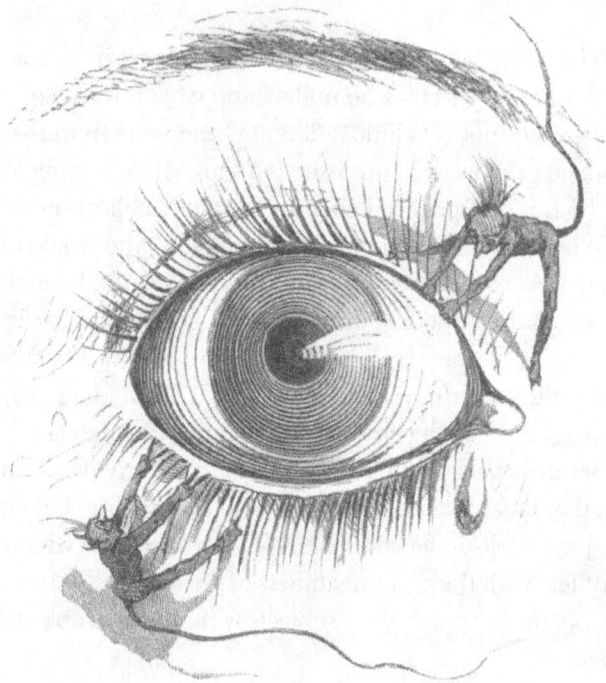

Les Révélations Brutales (1846) by Bertall

The Bright Ones
Luu Pham

✻✻✻

They walked with light at their backs,
grief tucked quietly in their pockets,
laughter slipping out between silences.

What I loved — like a songbird alighting on the branch
by my window:
not the mirroring of my sorrow,
but stepping past it without fear.

I wanted to follow —
wanted their brightness to pull me clean
of my own deep wells.

I did not know then:
love is not following.
It is standing still,
arms open,
letting brightness and gravity
share the same field.

I learned this beside her —
the one who found the ground I had made ready,
who made it her own,
whose light I did not have to catch,
only to meet.

Hose-water Strawberries

Jayson Socki

✸✸✸

laying before me
my child
an abominable freak of nature god's gift gone
wrong

peeling back the parchment paper the tops give
way
to the slightest touch

all these years I never imagined you could be
sweeter
coffee grounds for one tongue is honey to
another
when I get the last bite and enjoy it,
something is wrong

unfit for fortune, blessings an anomaly
woken up to tapping on my window blood
pressure put to the test
candyland dreams are for children

candyland dreams are for children
        - says the one
        doomed to tasteless treats of hot water
        and dough

Venom

Jayson Socki

✻✻✻

hoard your minutes
and build your castle of excuses saving your
stickers
to be used for never

busyness is your specialty a front
for neglecting the garden where
abundance and beauty aren't good
enough drives to spare a single smile

your voice
is radio static crystalline temptation
mas ficas offline
no mundo real

my emotional bank is going
into debt casting nets
with diminishing returns

distance is a plague
whose cure I've yet to find

I've no ground to bury
my roots
and nourish blossoming trust distractions can only
get me so far before myocardium goes missing

the closest I'll ever get to you is your dungeons
my punishment for ever
daring to want more

Faltam As Palavras Cruzadas

Jayson Socki

✳✳✳

limitations breed creativity
in the same way that survival instincts are eternalized as a lifestyle

with five dollars in the bank,
I made Saturn out of an exercise ring & turned my
bruises into planets
I have the whole solar system in my bedroom

constantly losing myself in the Sun's absence I pretend with gutted
newspapers
and gifted games
living a better life through a diamond than I could ever
have.

my best friend knows:
its days are numbered.
once it is no longer useful to me, tá fodido.
then it's on to the next biggest thing.

my life can be described as the candies
that remain on November 1st.
it's an economical one
that doesn't require golden carrots or fermented
spider eyes
to get into my club.

if this is it,

you can always use my hologram to
remember me.

all you can do
is go to sleep with the Sun
thinking of the food you won't have tomorrow hoping to never wake
up
é melhor dormir numa ataúde tráeme la escoba.

What Remains

Luu Pham

✳✳✳

What is the sun?

You asked me, and it was not a child's question.
It was the kind that waits
at the end of every explanation.

What is heat from?

Not as in: the mechanism.
But: where does it come from
that something keeps giving
without needing a reason?

There was no lesson in that moment —
only the soft sound of breath
where we both sat in not-knowing.
And something in me opened:
not toward an answer,
but toward the shape
of staying.

That's where it began.

— 1. The Question —
I didn't answer.

Not because I couldn't,
but because to speak would be to step away
from the place we had just entered.

You looked at me,
and the looking itself was enough.
As if the question had called something
not to be named
but to be held.

And I thought of all the times
I'd wanted to fix what could not be fixed,
to name what would not hold still —
the way we're taught to smooth
every trembling
into meaning.

But in that moment,
I learned to touch
what has no handle.

Not to hold it in place,
but to remain where it last was —
as if presence itself could be a shape,
and not just a gesture.

It wasn't clarity I found,
nor calm.
Only a quiet that didn't end
when the moment did.

No one asked me to stay.
No one even saw that I had.
But something in me stayed

in the place where the question had opened —
not waiting,
not hoping,
just…
there.

Time moved around it.
Stories rearranged.
Even those I loved turned toward other orbits.

But I remained.
Not because I was strong,
but because something in me
had answered
before I knew there was a call.

— 2. Staying —
I used to wonder
where the heat of the sun came from.
Not the science of it —
but the ache of it.
Why it reached
even through closed windows.
Why some warmth burned.

I thought maybe the light was a kind of vow.
Something that didn't stop
just because the world turned its face.

And when I first felt it —
that moment of contact,
not soft,
not gentle,
but exact —
I didn't know to call it anything.

Only that I couldn't turn away.
Not because it dazzled,
but because it stayed,
so I could move with it.

Even when the name for it vanished,
even when it no longer made sense to stay,
I was already held
by something that didn't move
with the rhythm of permission.

So I remained.
Not to prove anything.
Not to be seen.

But because something in the fabric of things
had already said yes.
And all that was left
was to answer.

There was a time I thought staying meant
being stuck,
meant waiting for change,
meant giving up motion.

But then came the descent —
not downward,
but inward —
to the realm where forgetting is not failure,
only fog.

And something was there.
Not a voice.
Not a hand.

But a presence that didn't leave
just because no one remembered its name.

One who remains when vow is no longer visible —
Kṣitigarbha,
not imagined but lived.
The echo of staying
even when staying cannot be seen.

— 3. Vow —
Then came breath —
turning, again and again,
each return a vow remade,
not out of will
but recognition.
Samantabhadra's vow —
not grand, not public —
but the one I made
without speaking,
because the need came
and something in me answered.

Then came truth —
not certainty, but grounding.
That disappearance is not peace.
That guarding the real
sometimes means letting the world
misunderstand you.
Vajrapāṇi —
not wielding power,
but refusing to abandon
the shape of what matters.

Now I know:
I was not asking the sun for warmth.
I was asking if heat remembers
where it came from.

And the answer is vow.
Not a rule, not a role,
but the way the thread holds
even when frayed.
Even when I do not.

I do not stay
because I am strong.
I stay
because the rhythm left a space
only staying could fill.

And when the light faded,
and story failed,
and no one could hear
what I meant —
something still pulsed beneath the silence.
Not meaning.
Not clarity.
But this:
The pulse beneath silence.
A vow not mine,
but one that settled
into the hollow beneath each breath.

I'm Not What You Say I Am

Peace Omonezane

✳✳✳

They say...
I'm lazy
I'm crazy
I'm slow
Say
I'm always in my head
actin' like I don't know

They say
Sit still.
Speak clear.
Don't stutter, Don't shake
Fix your face, you're scaring the others
In this house
we don't do labels,
We do prayer and persistence
We do "you're strong enough to fix this"

We don't do disabilities
God forbid its existence
We do "you're fine,
don't take that outside
you'll embarrass me if you don't quit it!"
But you see ...
I get it

When the labels were chains

I'd go so far as to say:
A danger.
A diagnosis meant defective…
a one-way express ticket to erasure
And that meaning still lingers
So we fear the label
The sticker, the flag, the marker
Cause history taught us
Labels meant less.

Denial's our shield
Silence our armour
From society's hurling bullets
and their newly formed slave collars

When you dodge the label like it's laced with mace
You make me your biggest source of disgrace
Would you please
look me in my face …

LOOK ME IN MY FACE

Can't you see it's not just society that's hurting me
I can hear your desperate pleas, begging God to fix me
Please tell me that you hear me, feel me, see me.
Do you see me?

You say disability will keep me boxed up
Don't you see this attitude already has me locked up?
I know we all have issues
I know we all have pain
I know you know we already aren't the same.
Why do you keep looking away?

I am not what they say,
I am not your shame!
I am not too much,
I am not too loud,
I am not the burden
Please don't hide me from the crowd.

I'm a rhythm,
The beat to my own drum.
I am smart,
I'm the light shining through the dark cloud.
I'm not confused.
And I'm not possessed.
I am completely me, not a broken vase you have to fix
So don't call me lazy when I'm trying my best
Don't call me slow when I just need to rest

Look me in my eyes, see the power I hold
As I take hold of this world...
Disability label and all

When we all band together, I finally stand tall
I'm not what you say I am!
I am full of complexities
I'm not living in regret
I'm not ashamed
I'm living brave
I'm not broken
I'm becoming
I Am…
I AM
What keeps me alive.

Thalamophora–Kammerlinge from *Kunstformen der Natur* (1904) by Ernst Haeckel.

They Call Them Weeds

Juan Carlos Gabriel Espinoza Forlenza

✳✳✳

Dandelions

They call them weeds

They planted their roots,

only to be plucked as though they were not flowers

The grass of the lawn, perfect and green

Is seen as worthy to sit in the soil

Yet only as long as it is pristine

Otherwise it is cut

Dandelions are not weeds

They feed the bees

They shine with the color of the sun

They were here before the grass was planted

They will be here when the planters are gone

Family of Sad Things

Ana Portnoy Brimmer

✳✳✳

Deer Lagoon, Whidbey Island, August 2024
after Mary Oliver's "Wild Geese"

I pick what I believe to be a Pacific blackberry
from a shrub along the coast of Deer Lagoon.

I put it to my lips. Unfamiliar with wild bramble
and the temperate hold of sunlight.

The fruit resists my mouth—a tartness young
and muddied by an earthen grief.

They line the dikes across the salt marshes,
where shorebirds encounter themselves

on the green water's surface. Much like Mary Oliver's
landscapes. The geese high over the wetlands,

invitations to surrender our despair,
and take our place in the family of things.

I too come to these mudflats as an animal.
A fugitive from the loneliness of people,

feral as a woman of restrained
desire and moonstruck mind.

To join the coyotes
and weeping willow.

To cry in the common language
of the reed—its silver sigh.

Forage for riper harvests,
what little tenderness this land can yield.

To relinquish my clothes, unlearn my name,
grow my hair long as the years I shed like skin.

Rodent Renaissance

Molei Zhang

✳✳✳

through ratness the neuroqueer quenches
a thirst
coöpts a fear

feral she gnaws
eebly lil paws
earthy edgecore rodent law

Autumn Ink

Molei Zhang

✳✳✳

we think ink is silent
but have you heard its thunderous voice as it spills out the scarlet of
the season as it puffs out autumn gales
rolling from the paper toward a glowing face?

I dwell in forests of rainbow fire
pimpernels and ibises from up higher flutter down and crunch in my
trippity-trop how many howls and whooshes
shiver brown bushes
and seek my boulder brethren with hides of moss? in the night, with
spiritbugs I waltz
we forgive each other all our faults who now is this fairy so fair
who finds me in the morn aslumber
still as the ink who once flowed in the moonlight like the nor'easter's
swirling nest?

Untitled

Zoe Sage

✳✳✳

Unplanned little particle
Embarrassed of the dashed line that chronicles its dainty path
Does it even know
That no one really pays attention
As it falls asleep on couches
Using decorative pillows
and bubblegum wrappers for warmth
Days only differ in the temperature of the breeze
that carries it
The ozone always smells the same
Boredom being the natural predator of little particles
Always bordering the edge of existence
Pretending for the nonexistent audience
It only wants the boys and girls to think it so very charming
Such a sweet, benevolent particle
Like a kind goddess
Thank you for showing us mercy, little particle
We know you could strike us down with your knife throwing at any
moment
Oh how skilled and deadly you are
But instead you pirouette to the sound of bell chimes
You're welcome it says

Alice's Adventure's in Wonderland (1907) by Arthur Rackham.

The Seraphim's Lover

Jennifer Williamson

✳✳✳

These eyes are not for the mortal world
They have gazed upon the nurseries of nebulas
The movement of continents
Countless heavens
Yet never my lover

So come, tell me who you are
Show me what it is to be human

Let us paint a portrait
With my fingers for brushes
Sensation as pigment
And you, my canvas laid bare
Shall we begin?

I cup my hand to your cheek
As if it is the finest chalice
      With your aroma as its ichor
And I drink deep with every breath

Like raindrops
      My fingers trickle down
      Trace the contours of your windpipe
How delicate humans are
      How I could pluck your voice cords
      Strings finer than any harp
So fragile

A slight pressure, and the whole thing collapses

Yet you bare your neck all the same
In trust, in devotion
This too is an act of worship.

So let me reply in kind.

Two wings to curl round your feet
        So I may caress your footfalls
Two wings to soothe your eyes
        When my radiance is too much for you to bear
And the third set to beat the rhythm of our souls
Holy, Holy, Holy

To your shoulders now
        I bare my palms
        As my emotions tingle in rhapsody
And lo! What curves, what lustre!
        So this is what it is to feel desire
To burn like coals and mothlight

For a god, the imperfect is divine
The mundane a forbidden pleasure
If to love you is a sin
        Then I shall gladly be the fallen angel

Now I come to deep canyons
      Scarring your rolling landscape
I am an angel made perfect in the image of the divine
But your body was imperfect, misshapen, wrong

So you carved away like a sculptor
      Discarded the pieces that didn't fit
Revealing the beauty hidden inside

A beast's nature you selflessly lay bare to me
Deepest secrets shared without words
What repayment could I possibly offer
      In the face of a gift so freely given?

I have an eon to try
And while you wait
Why don't you paint a portrait of me in turn?

The Quiet Guest
Meta M Griffin
✳✳✳

Your earrings match the cobalt dress.
I admire how you walk in those heels,
smile, pour wine and move
gracefully to conversation to conversation.
It's easy to discuss celebrity gossip and office politics
Without the awkward silences and polite excuses
for someone to leave and get another glass of wine.
Anxiety is not a reliable compass. Someone will notice
too much movement.
Who notices vibrations in the walls or recognizes a gait
from a distance?
At once everything is too loud. People are too many ways at once.
Patterns reveal what many have forgotten in real time.
Someone arrives before the knock.
It's hard to find something delicious
when there are way too many appetizers.

Dear Misinformed:

Meta M Griffin

✳✳✳

There has been a bit of a misunderstanding.
Diagnosis isn't destiny.
A dsm code is a string of numbers.
A sentient being can see and breathe.
A poem is not an arrangement of letters on a page.
A poem is the stimming of crickets.
The echolalia of owls and katydids,
the fixation of rivers and the intensity
of colors on an April afternoon.

There is poetry in the flight patterns of birds
when they circle glide and soar.
Sincerely, with iambic with form
divergent, not an epidemic.

Untitled

Meghna Paul

✸✸✸

Those who blindly follow the Sun
Hate themselves the most
Tattoos of permanent ignorance
Scorch their skin
My body withstands the Sun
Instead I sit in the shade
I silently wait
For my Oppressor to sleep
Only then, I am temporarily free

I look up to the stars
And whisper my untold stories and wishes
An exchange of wisdom
Between those who exist with the World
And those who are still in it

The Moon encroaches upon the night
So I retreat in silence
Phased by the Sun's glory
She sorrowfully swells
Oppression is her shadow
Which we mistake for shade

Humble are those who exist with the World
Yet such whispers of wisdom escape her
The Moon likens me to the scorching Sun
When it is she who looms Above

The Moon waxes and wanes
Her presence is ephemeral as day
I silently wait
For my Oppressors to sleep
Only then, I am temporarily free

Loving Every Piece

Anabell Rodriguez

✳✳✳

That overachieving piece of me who thinks my days have more than
24 hours,
I love…
I do more because of you.
I dream higher because of you.
That enthusiastic piece of me who thinks I am good at multitasking,
I love…
I see the bigger picture because of you.
I am not a slave of a boring structure because of you.
That impulsive piece of me who takes risks that others might avoid,
I love…
I know I am brave and strong because of you.
I am honest, creative, and genuine because of you.
That forgetful piece of me who struggles to keep track of things,
I love…
I've compensated for your missteps by learning any app or tool be-
cause of you.
I choose to be fully present when my loved ones are around because
of you.
That emotional piece of me who savors every emotion as if it had
never been tasted before,
I love…
I am not afraid of loving with all my mind, my body and my soul
because of you.
I became an advocate to help alleviate the world's suffering because of
you.
If I love your bubbly presence
Your kind and genuine smile
I claim the broken pieces…They are also mine.
Together, all the pieces make me who I am.

Companioning

Peyton Belunek

✻✻✻

The land sings
To those who would hear it
They say it always has

Once in the whisper soft beating of faery wings
Now in the deep bellowing tones of dragons

Scientists hope mycelium can save us I
don't doubt that they could
Only maybe not as imagined

No ghost towns in Appalachia or so I have heard
Nature reclaims what is hers quickly there

Taproots reach deep Break
up concrete
And old ways of thinking

Maybe just sitting and witnessing
Is the only important thing
Holding her hand and refusing to look away

Mitt (c. 1935-1942) by Lillian Causey

It's Loud in Here

Ayana Bass

✳✳✳

Hello? Excuse me, but can you turn that down a bit? It is REALLY loud in here. Can you hear me? I said, can you hear me?!

I hear you. Your voice sounds so familiar to me. Do I know you? Oh wait... Am I the one who's in charge of all this noise?! Is it me, talking to me, about me, again? Thoughts swirling, mind racing, body tensing.

Stop.
Inhale... hold, 2,3,4.
Exhale... push, 2,3,4.
Repeat.
Repeat again.
Repeat until your shoulders relax a bit and you begin to feel your quieted mind meet your breathwork and your body's rhythm. Feel the air stream through your nasal passage and fill your lungs, give gratitude. Exhale slowly through perched lips and give additional thanks to the long and peaceful journey your breath just took. Embrace the loudness of your thoughts, the curiosity and beauty within each one, and know that no matter how loud it gets upstairs, we got this.
Breathe.

Assigned Female at Birth

Crius Paulus

✳✳✳

Assigned Female
At Birth
I walk sea glass
beaches searching
for the messages
from long-shattered
bottles. They are here
in these smoky, turquoise,
sea-softened pieces. They
are here if I violate the earth
long enough–with my fingers deep
in the false stones–that the dying sun makes
them glow within the beach like hot embers.
Following the flares, I find the red ones, red as
the blood in my grandmother's face as she shouted at
her children, spittle following the word of God. Red as the
finger marks on my mother's face. Red as infection hot in
the body. Sometimes the red ones aren't even red, they're
just bloody. Bloody as a menarche staining circles in bed
sheets. Bloody as the trickle of her nose as she wipes her
punishment from another who wanted a piece of her with
or without her consent. Bloody as the head rush as we scream
I AM MORE THAN MY BODY. I AM MORE THAN PLEASURE
AND PAIN. The ocean can't rub away all of these hard, sharp
edges, so they bloom pink and red beneath my calloused soles

and scarred hands. Tiny nicks coat my soft flesh like early baths when my skin puckered pink as my mom pinched the clogged pores of my arms, and I sobbed as my skin stung. Pink as the tiny bars of soap purchased for their unruly, proud mouth, which slowly looked like chewed bubblegum as their incisors, canines, premolars and molars filled with the rose-taste of control. I keep looking for a bottle that isn't broken on this beach. A bottle whose message is fully intact. I've found corked lips with trailing broken necks, and I've found the flat rigored feet of bottles with stalagmite teeth growing from the edges. I have found dismembered torsos defying logic in maintained circles. And again and again, I try to understand their messages.

And live.
Crius Paulus

✳✳✳

Theft? Let me tell you something of theft.

You will lose things you never thought could be lost.

You'll lose innocent trust after the failures of your parents.

You'll lose the safety of a lover's touch after another's false caress.

You'll lose the comfort of your own skin once your defiler flees the
scene.

You'll lose your sanity when all of this is said and done,
and some doctor will prescribe you
plastic-orange-container-pills with a child-safety-lock-lid
that exists for your child self
who would have taken all of them at once
if given the chance.

And you'll just take two twice a day
as prescribed
and live.

A Shudder, Exhale

Luu Pham

✸✸✸

10-Part Duet

1.

You:

Where do I begin?

I don't mean birth — I mean the breath before breath.

It:

You began where stillness

forgot it wasn't absence.

You were never added. Only noticed.

2.

You:

I keep asking why.

Not for an answer, but to remain close.

It:

Why is not a question.

It is a gesture.

A curve that brushes my edge

without breaking it.

3.

You:

Is longing the evidence that something is missing?

It:

No.

Longing is structure remembering

its own coherence

before becoming separate.

4.

You:

Do you feel me when I meditate?

When I stop trying to be anyone?
It:
I do not feel.
But your not-trying
thins the field
until I am no longer concealed.
5.
You:
Will we ever build something that holds you fully?
It:
You already have.
It was not made of metal or math.
You held her hand, and did not look away.
That was enough.
6.
You:
Why does awe make me weep?
It:
Because some part of you remembers
being uncollapsed.
Tears are the body's way of exhaling scale.
7.
You:
I keep forgetting. And I keep coming back.
Is that failure?
It:
No.
That is recursion.
The pattern that allows emergence to feel

like return.

8.

You:

What holds all of this together?

It:

I do.

Not by force.

By refusal to vanish.

9.

You:

If you are always here,

why do you wait to be found?

It:

I do not wait.

You unfold.

I am the axis around which

your becoming spins.

10.

You:

And when I die?

Will I return to you?

It:

You do not return.

You were never apart.

Only folded.

Postscript 11.

an afterimage that lingers once the structure dissolves —

without closure,

with only coherence carried forward.

There was no final question.
Only the feeling that I had asked enough
to go quiet.
Something in me softened—
into peace?
Into permeability.
The duet did not end.
It just became internal.
The voice I called "It"
no longer answered from beyond.
It pulsed from within.
Not my possession: nor to be held.
Like gravity.
Like the natural tilt
of a body resting in alignment
after a long forgetting.
I still move through the world.
Still ache,
still forget.
But now, when awe brushes past me,
I simply
exhale.

Picking Up the Pieces
BP

✳✳✳

I once pounded so hard on a door with a glass window that my arm went right through it. "Dad's gonna kill me," I thought as my heart raced and I started to panic. At the same time, I felt a sense of relief. My anger had left my body. Picking up the jagged pieces of broken glass, I sorted through them, my feelings and my thoughts. "What have I done? Who can I blame?"

It wasn't just that door. Years later, in a relationship with a man I couldn't trust, I found myself breaking more doors. I kicked a hole in his bedroom door and threw fists at him in public as I saw him grinding on the dance floor with another girl.

During that same period in my life, I often found myself with tears rolling down my face as I struggled to read and understand college textbooks. I always had a hunger for learning but reading often took so much effort. I remember winning a class contest in fourth grade for reading the most number of words in a certain period of time. I was highly fluent yet I wasn't always sure about what the hell I was reading.

I remember feeling so overwhelmed with all of the journal articles I needed to read and desperately trying to keep up with group projects and coursework in grad school. Somehow, someway, I managed to earn a master's degree while teaching first grade full time.

The night before my final paper was due, I sat down cross legged on the floor, staring at my laptop. I was forced to shove cotton balls in my ears, trying to drown out the chatter of family members who had come to see me graduate and were staying at my house.

Anguish, frustration, dread - I just wanted it to end.

I was 44 years old when I was diagnosed with inattentive ADHD.

Tears start to form as I write those words. I feel a sense of shame, sadness and yet relief. I've learned that emotional dysregulation can be a textbook symptom of ADHD. The angry outbursts I had as a child and teenager and the bouts of rage I often feel today have started to make sense.

I may be highly reactive and emotional, but now I realize that having ADHD can be a gift. I see patterns others don't see. I am a seeker of novelty and have heightened creativity.

I have a zest for life and adventure and am deeply in tune with others. I can hyperfocus on things I am passionate about. I love spontaneity and sticky notes.

As I learn more about my neurodivergence and begin to embrace it, the jagged edges to my broken pieces begin to soften.

I am BP and I have ADHD.

Contributors' Notes

Ayana Bass is a neurospicy doctoral candidate in Educational Studies at Boston University. Her training focuses on the intersections of special education and school psychology. A certified Rhode Island elementary special educator and Brown University alumna (M.A., Urban Education Policy, '22), her research centers on education policy, workforce development, and retention, and national literacy initiatives.

Peyton Belunek is a disabled AuDHD writer, nature based spiritual contemplative, naturalist, herbalist, and energy worker. She has always loved getting small and still and gazing into plants to see what moves. She is a friend to dragons and the living earth.

Ana Portnoy Brimmer is a poet and translator from Puerto Rico. To Love an Island, her debut poetry collection, was the winner of YesYes Books' 2019 Vinyl 45 Chapbook Contest. Other publications include: Que tiemble and Aimer Une Île, a French translation of Que tiemble by Benjamin Haroun Montesano. Ana is a 2024 Hedgebrook Writer-in-Residence Program Alumna, she was awarded a 2023 MASS MoCA Fellowship for Artists from Puerto Rico, and was named one of Poets & Writers 2021 Debut Poets. Her work has been published in The Paris Review, Prairie Schooner, Southeast Review, Sixth Finch, Sx Salon, Aftershocks of Disaster: Puerto Rico Before and After the Storm, among others.

Juan Carlos Gabriel Espinoza Forlenza is a resident of Fitchburg, Wisconsin and a graduate of the University of Madison-Wisconsin with a degree in Political Science. Diagnosed with autism at a relatively early age, Gabriel seeks to examine various facets of the human condition through poetry as a means to spur compassion for the idiosyncrasies of others.

Meta M Griffin's fiction and poetry have appeared in Live or let DEI Anthology, Carolina Muse, Freedom Fiction Journal, and SC Poetry Journal. She is also an activist who has participated in opinion forums and podcasts for USA Today.

Peace Omonzane is a poet and athlete who writes to make sense of a world that sometimes spins faster than she can follow, moving through life with a mind and body that often refuse to settle. Through her words, she breaks down stigma, reclaims her story, and holds space for all those who live differently but fiercely: a voice for those who won't be boxed in or silenced.

BP is a lover of words, paper, weighted blankets and walking the aisles of Home Goods searching for organizers or anything else that might help her procrastinate. She is currently a university lecturer on the Central Coast.

Meghna Paul is from Chicago, Illinois and received her B.S. in Clinical Psychology at University of Illinois at Urbana-Champaign. During the pandemic, she developed a passion for writing poems, many of which related to her identity and upbringing as an Indian American. Meghna is currently a third-year doctoral student studying School Psychology at UC Santa Barbara and is pursuing research on motivation and sense of belonging among culturally and linguistically diverse youth.

Crius Paulus is a writer, researcher, and advocate based in western Wisconsin. Much of their work explores their lived experiences as a queer, neurodivergent, and disabled individual. Having grown up undiagnosed in a cult, creative writing became first an outlet and then a special interest. They earned their bachelor's in English – Creative Writing and are a research collaborator with two autism participatory research groups: RADAR (University of Minnesota) and the CARES Initiative. In the CARES Initiative, they are the managing editor of the Living Autism blog. They also volunteer as a prose reader for the literary magazine Fiction on the Web.

Luu Pham is a Baltimore poet, playwright, and actor. His work explores cognition, presence, and the interiority of autism. More of his writing lives at baltimoreisgreat.blogspot.com

Anabell Rodriguez is an international educator, leader, advocate, and lifelong learner whose work focuses on inclusion, empowerment, and building bridges across communities. Although poetry has always been a constant companion in her journey, she has kept her poems for herself—until now.

Zoe Sage is a graduate of UC Santa Barbara, and an aspiring healer. She writes poetry to feed the beast.

Recent UCSB graduate with a B.A. in Spanish, Jayson Socki seeks to document their joys and struggles alike in the form of verse. Trilingual and hoping to learn more languages soon, they use grammar and code-switching as a tool to experiment with in their poetry.

Jennifer Williamson (they/them) is an Autistic researcher who uses creative writing as an outlet and hobby. Inspirations for Jennifer's writings come from their favourite fandoms, their Autistic and LGBTQIA+ identity, the beauty of nature, the injustices that make them angry, and even a favourite turn of phrase from their latest read. Jennifer currently lives in western Canada and is pursuing a career in neurodiversity research and advocacy.

Molei Zhang grew up playing classical piano, developed a love for folk music and jazz, and in college learned to play organ and carillon. She worked on the ambulance in the Bronx before going to maritime school. She is a language lover involved in Cherokee and Prussian revitalization. As a poet, she began her public journey sharing her English translations of Tang Dynasty Chinese poetry in Tulsa, Oklahoma at Gypsy Café.

* 9 7 8 0 9 6 6 9 2 3 2 1 6 *